Be Your own damn Hero!

Coloring Book for Strong Women

© 2021 by Sweet Harmony Press. All right reserved. No part of this publication may be reproduced, stored in a retrieval system, stored in a database and / or published in any form or by any means, electronic, mechanical, photocopying, recording or otherwise, without the
prior written permission of the publisher.

For inquiries for bulk or wholesale orders, contact info@sweetharmonypress.com

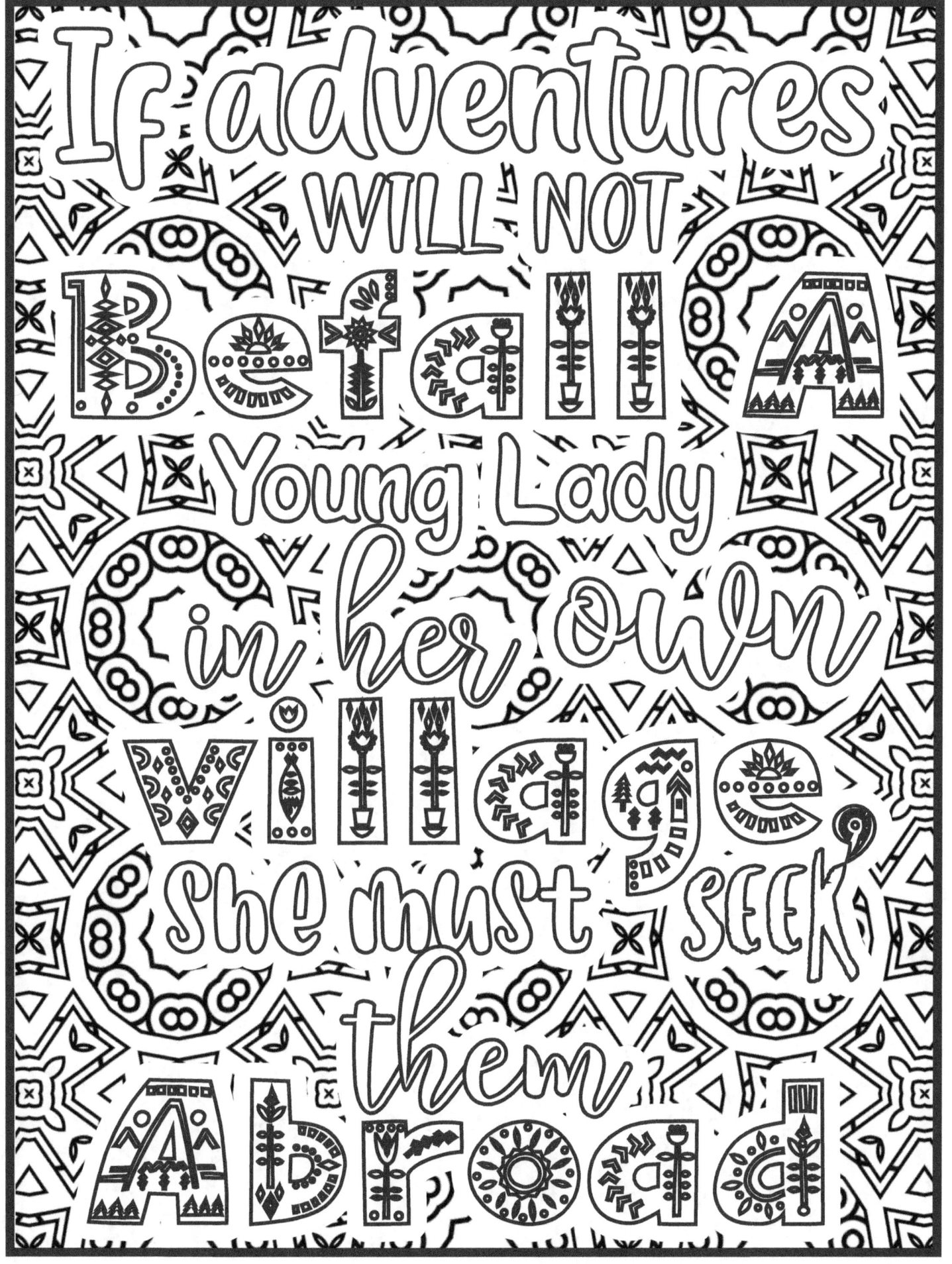

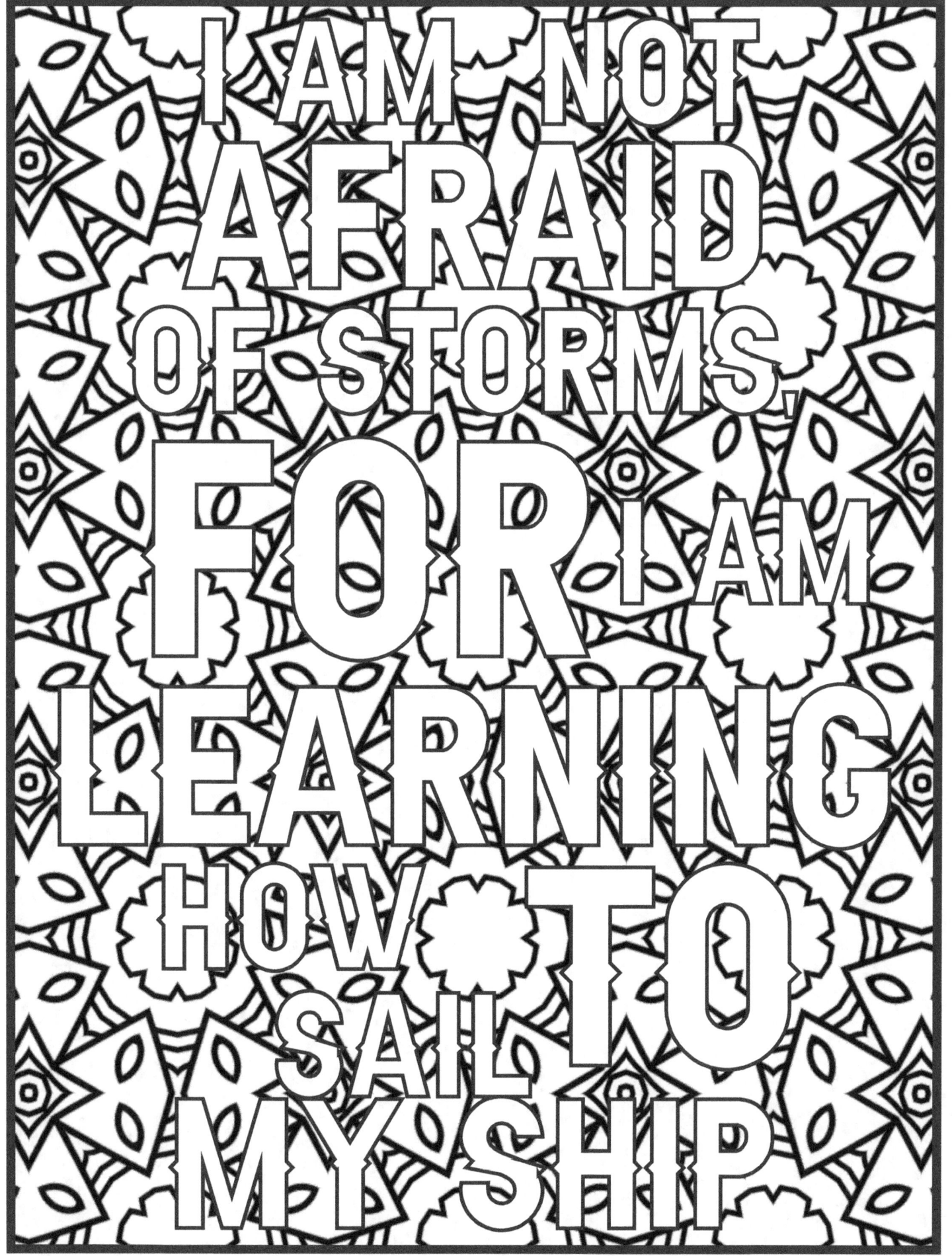

www.ingramcontent.com/pod-product-compliance
Lightning Source LLC
Chambersburg PA
CBHW081755100526
44592CB00015B/2448